MODEL TANKS

Tom Cole

AMBERLEY

First published 2021

Amberley Publishing
The Hill, Stroud
Gloucestershire, GL5 4EP

www.amberley-books.com

Copyright © Tom Cole, 2021

The right of Tom Cole to be identified as
the Author of this work has been asserted in
accordance with the Copyrights, Designs and
Patents Act 1988.

ISBN 978 1 4456 7971 6 (print)
ISBN 978 1 4456 7972 3 (ebook)

British Library Cataloguing in Publication Data.
A catalogue record for this book is available from
the British Library.

Origination by Amberley Publishing.
Printed in the UK.

Contents

Introduction   4

Model Making in History   5

A Question of Scale   12

Practical Tips for Making Better Models   25

Detailing Your Models   36

Painting and Finishing Your Model   44

First World War and the Interwar Period   56

Second World War – British Armoured Vehicles   65

Second World War – German Armoured Vehicles   77

Modern Tanks   85

Where Next?   93

Last Words   96

Introduction

When Amberley Books first approached me about writing *Model Tanks* I asked if they wanted twelve volumes or if they thought I should get it down to a mere ten. When they said it would be a single book, and a slim one at that, it became clear that I would only be able to scratch the surface of the subject. Another concern I had was that, as a life-long modeller in small scale, I was aware that I would have little to say about the current most popular scale of 1/35. While there are a few examples of the dominant scale within these pages I make no apologies for the emphasis being on 1/76 and 1/72. Much has been written online, in commercial magazines and on the printed page about 1/35 scale, so I hope the reader finds the prominence of small scale refreshing. I also touch on a scale that is sadly neglected. I built Bandai 1/48 scale models in the 1970s and recall they were beautifully detailed. The modern Tamiya offerings in this scale are of an even better standard. The problem is that the range is very limited. It is almost like being back in the 1970s when the number of military models was very limited and to extend the range you had to resort to converting and scratch-building. That brings me on to my final point. As well as a canter through the wonderful world of model tanks, the early chapters of the book takes the reader on a journey – my journey in model making. From Wargaming models as a teenager through to rediscovering the hobby after a long absence, it is no exaggeration to say the hobby has changed my life. This is my third published book and I have a large circle of good friends through gluing bits of plastic together! Almost incidentally my knowledge and skills have greatly improved.

It's a wonderful hobby and if it is new to you or you are returning after a long absence, then I hope *Model Tanks* helps you along the path of enjoying military model making.

Tom Cole

Model Making in History

Model making has been around for possibly as long as civilisation itself. Models of soldiers and ships have been found in ancient Egyptian tombs and throughout the generations architectural models have been used to show how a building, town or city will look. Up until the Second World War models tended to be in the realm of the rich. Metal soldiers depicting the Soldiers of Empire adorned the bedrooms of boys of the affluent classes, as did early tin plate trains and ships. But it was after the Second World War when boys of all social classes gained access to models and model making. This revolution was brought about by a new media: plastic.

It seems almost impossible now to imagine a world without plastics. They are omnipresent to the point where concern about the oceans clogging with plastic is a major area of worry for most that care about the planet. Yet before the Second World War plastic, as we know it, was virtually unknown. Airfix founder Nicholas Kove realised shortly after the Second World War that the future lay in plastics and he was one of the pioneers of the process of forming the plastic into shapes, known as injection moulding.

Airfix in the Early Days

Airfix was founded in 1939 by Hungarian entrepreneur Nicholas Kove. While it would be satisfying to think that the name was derived from the company's most famous products (AIRcraft being FIXed together), the truth is far more mundane. Mr Kove's company made rubber-based air-filled toys. 'Fixed' with air the canny Kove wanted the company name to start with an 'A' so that it would appear at the start of any trade directories. Hence Airfix. The first model kit as we would recognise it was a 1/20 scale Ferguson Tractor (the initial models were provided as built models for owner Harry Ferguson as promotional pieces). However, Nicholas Kove saw the potential of a kit of parts that could be assembled by the customer. Stocked by FW Woolworths, the Ferguson kit was joined in 1952 by a tiny model of Sir Francis Drake's famous ship, the *Golden Hind*. Although currently only available second hand, this little iconic kit would remain in production for many years.

Airfix – Educator to the Masses

There can be little doubt that for many boys (and girls) Airfix helped develop skills and provide knowledge that would last a lifetime. Hand and artistic skills would develop through putting together and painting models. But perhaps more importantly the model makers would be spurred on to know more about the subjects they were modelling, and their context and place in history. For many, lifelong interests in aircraft, warships, and military vehicles, as well as motor cars, sailing ships and historical figures, would develop as a result of building kits. For example, the unusual asymmetrical Second World War German reconnaissance plane, the Blohm and Voss BV 141, consisting of a straight, wide wing with a narrow fuselage, with an engine at one end and tail plane at the other, but positioned off centre with a nacelle looking like a bizarre greenhouse housing the crew on the opposite side. This unusual arrangement would have given the crew great all-round vision – ideal for a reconnaissance aircraft. However, only ten were ever built so it was not an aircraft that made a great contribution to the German war effort. Yet because Airfix released a model of the BV 141 in 1970s, it is well known by model makers, giving it a fame that is hardly justified by its service history.

The Airfix kit of the German BV 141. An obscure Second World War reconnaissance aircraft that is probably only well known because of the Airfix kit of the 1970s.

The Airfix brand produced some wonderful drawings to inspire model makers but often they were not always historically accurate, as this 'Afrika Korps' Panther shows.

Although Airfix can be viewed as triggering interest in military aircraft, vehicles and tanks, they did not always get it right. I well remember a lively discussion at school with like-minded friends about the use of the German Panther tank in the Western Desert. The header card for the Airfix series one kit showed a Panther in a desert setting (with a burning ambulance in the background), so it must have been part of the Afrika Korps. However, the first Panthers did not enter service until the battle of Kursk in July 1943 – some two months after the Germans had been finally defeated in North Africa.

Growing up with Airfix

Airfix lead the charge for what would be termed the Golden Age of Model Making in the 1960s and 1970s. When a teenager in Grimsby in the 1970s I lived no more than a twenty-minute cycle ride away from five shops that sold construction kits. Favourite was the 'Dolls Hospital'. This was a proper local model shop, suitably stacked from floor to ceiling with boxes and bags of construction kits. A five-minute cycle away from there was Gregory's Cycle Shop that carried a small selection of kits – mostly Airfix. Twenty minutes in the other direction in Cleethorpes was Loftus Model Railway shop. While, not unnaturally, it mainly stocked model railways, the shop had a good selection of kits. Perhaps the best shop for stock and variety (particularly around Christmas) was the toy department in the Ron Ramsden's department store. Closest, but with the smallest number of kits, was the local hardware shop. The name escapes me but it was

The local model shop was always a source of excitement. Most are sadly gone but the Ely Cycle Centre has a well-stocked model shop that is well worth a visit.

known as the 'Paraffin Shop' because my Dad would visit on a regular basis to fill up a small tin with paraffin that, in the days before central heating, was used as the fuel for a couple of heaters that sat in the dining room and on the first floor landing to 'take the chill off' the bedrooms. Further afield in the town centre was FW Woolworths (Woolies) and WH Smiths, both of which had carousels that displayed most, if not all, of the Airfix series one and two kits.

Wargaming

Like many youngsters of the Airfix generation, I collected model soldiers. Not the big expensive metal ones from Britains but the HO/OO soft plastic figures from Airfix. supplemented by a Dinky Centurion. I developed a rudimentary 'war game' that involved lining up the figures and flicking marbles at them across the carpet. The discovery in the local library of Terence Wise's *Introduction to Battle Gaming* was a revelation. The marbles were gone forever to be replaced with dice, a tape measure and

Wargaming was a popular hobby in the 1970s and Airfix had a vast range of soldiers to fill the ranks of many small-scale armies. Here some First World War French infantry charge forward.

The Dinky range of military models were simple diecast toys and although not to the same scale as the Airfix figures they were part of the author's first wargaming army.

Terry Wise's book *Introduction to Battle Gaming* inspired many junior Generals, including the author.

scenery. Airfix became my armourer with a growing interest in the Second World War being fuelled by my first military vehicle (a Sherman) and this was soon accompanied by more Shermans, Half Tracks and Carriers with artillery support from 25 pounders and 5.5' Gun/Howitzers. With a small army assembled I decided to join the Grimsby Horse and Musket Society (coincidently located above the 'Paraffin Shop' mentioned earlier). Monday night was club night and I quickly learnt that I knew very little about wargaming or model making. With the help and advice from other enthusiasts, who specialised in the Second World War, my model making skills improved greatly. However, this would all end on 3 January 1978 when I joined the Royal Air Force.

Return to the Hobby

A long and busy career in the RAF, and bringing up three children, took away most of my spare time, so my model making sat firmly on the back burner for around twenty-seven years. However, with a more sedate job in 'Civvy Street', and the children dispatched to work and university, I found myself with time on my hands. I returned to the hobby in 2005 and found it was a very different pastime. Military modelling was now dominated by 1/35 scale vehicles. Japanese firm Tamiya had released their 1/35 scale Panther in 1962 and within a few years the large-scale kits overtook the smaller 1/76 and 1/72 scale kits from Airfix and Revell.

Today the Airfix brand is almost as strong as it was in the heydays of the 1970s. Some of the kits, particularly the large-scale aircraft like the Mosquito and Typhoon, are world leaders and rightly popular. In small scale, many of the military vehicles are no longer in production. In the 2018 Airfix catalogue the 1/76 scale vehicles had all but disappeared, but a change of heart in mid-2018 saw a change of direction and most of the small-scale vehicles reappeared in the 'Classic Kit' range.

While small-scale models dominated the 1960s and early 1970s, the arrival of 1/35 scale kits in the mid-1970s would quickly dominate the model making market. Shown is an early Tamiya King Tiger box art.

Although many of the Airfix kits are over fifty years old they are still popular and Airfix have re-released many in their 'Classic Kit' range. Picture and contents remained the same over the decades, but the packaging changed.

A Question of Scale

If you are returning to the hobby, or just starting out, the first question you might want to answer is in which scale shall I build my models? Some modellers choose to model in a variety of scales, but most have a favourite and seldom stray from it. I have always modelled in small scale, predominately 1/76 but recently I have enjoyed building models in 1/72 and have dipped a cautious toe in 1/48 scale, but more of this later. Let's take a look at the variety of scales from the micro tank to the life size.

1/300 and 1/285

Predominately, this scale is used for wargaming. Normally cast in white metal, early models were little more than 'micro-blobs' and it was difficult to distinguish between a Panzer I and Tiger tank. However, some have taken these tiny models to a new level and the standard of models from companies like GHQ has set a very high standard when you consider that the figures used are only 6 mm tall.

1/144 and 1/150

These equate to railway N gauge. PG Models produce a superb range of modern vehicles that are aimed at railway modellers looking to populate their layouts with military vehicles. They also fit in well with the ever-growing range of 1/144 scale aircraft and one of the big model manufacturers Revell have produced a couple of sets in this small scale.

1/100

This is a very popular scale for wargaming. Figures are 15 mm high and the Plastic Soldier Company produce a large range of vehicles and figures. Russia-based Zvezda also produce simplified vehicles in this scale as part of their 'Art of Tactic' wargame.

1/87

Many of the military vehicle scales can trace their roots in railway modelling and 1/87 is the dominant model railway scale in Europe. It is also known as HO, which means

PG Models make tanks in pewter that fit in with N gauge railways (1/152 scale).

Aircraft modellers have used 1/144 scale for some time, but the scale has never caught on with military vehicle modellers.

An increasingly popular scale for wargaming is 1/100, which Russian company Zvezda use as part of their 'Art of Tactic' wargames system.

Half 'O' (more on that later). Minitank by Roco used to produce a vast array of tanks and soft skins. Like in the model railway world 1/87 was never popular in the UK.

1/76

This scale equates to 4 mm to the foot which has its origins in the model railway scale of 'OO' gauge. There is a thought that Airfix produced their range of military vehicles in 1/76 to go with their range of figures and model railway, rather than 1/72 which was their main aircraft scale. The dominant manufacturers were Airfix and Matchbox (with Revell now running some of the Matchbox kits alongside their

A popular scale for the model railway builder in Europe, 1/87 has never really caught on in the UK. This Tiger from Minitanks is one of the few readily available. (Photograph by Alex Cossey)

Although Airfix aircraft were mainly 1/72, their military vehicle range was to 1/76 scale. Japanese companies Nitto and Fujimi followed this trend. This is an example from Fujimi of a Tiger I. (Photograph by Alex Cossey)

1/72 range). Japan-based Fujimi and Nitto produced military vehicle kits in 1/76 but apart from them and a few minor manufacturers most other large injection-moulded plastic companies produce kits in 1/72. Airfix have recently re-released most of their 1/76 range under the 'Classic Kit' label, no doubt aimed at those nostalgic for the older kits. Some of these Airfix kits are over fifty years old and it shows! However, Airfix have recently produced some excellent kits in this scale and with a little work even the old kits can be brought up to a reasonable standard. These kits were popular with wargamers (author included) as there was nothing else.

1/72

Undoubtedly the most popular scale in the smaller scales. The early kits from one of the early manufacturers – Esci – emerged a little after the early Airfix kits and they set the standard for small-scale modelling. That tradition of high-quality kits has continued, with the major manufacturers Revell, Dragon and Italeri producing some incredibly detailed kits in 1/72. Some manufacturers have produced military vehicles in this scale aimed at the wargamer. There tends to be two 'snap together' kits in the box with the emphasis being on a sturdy model that can withstand frequent handling on the wargames table, rather than having large amounts of fine detail. Zvezda have bucked that particular trend by producing wargames models that are highly detailed.

Russian manufacturer Zvezda have expanded their range of 1/72 military kits recently and cover a range of subjects with high quality kits. Here is their early production Tiger I. (Photograph by Alex Cossey)

Dragon are well known for their large-scale kits but their kits in small scale offer a high level of detail. Their unique 'DS' tracks are easy to fit and look the part. Dragon late version Tiger I, complete with Zimmerit finish. (Photograph by Alex Cossey)

The main advantage of the smaller scales is that they do not take up a lot of space. The 1/72 Sherman and LCM 3 shown take up less than a third of the space filled by the same vehicles in 1/35. Models by Simon Ward.

1/56

Another scale like 1/100 (which is aimed at the wargamer) is also known as 28mm as this is the height of the figures. Kits from the major manufacturers like Italeri tend to be simplified (for example suspension units and tracks are produced as a single item).

1/48

Also known as 'Quarter Scale' this is a very popular scale for model aircraft manufacturers but, aside from a few kits from Bandai in the 1970s and todays offerings from Tamiya, it is not a popular scale for military vehicle model makers. The issue has been partially addressed by some great models from Accurate Armour, but they are mainly soft skins based around aircraft subjects. It is a good compromise – more detailed than 1/72 but doesn't take up the space of 1/35 scale – but there is just not the range of vehicles to make it popular.

Another kit designed for wargamers, but this time in 1/56 scale from Italeri. The scale often quoted is 28 mm – this being the height of the average soldier in 1/56 scale. (Photograph by Alex Cossey)

Another scale that is popular with aircraft modellers but has yet to catch on in a big way for military model makers is 1/48. Here is an example from Tamiya of a Tiger I. (Photograph by Alex Cossey)

1/32

Known by some as the 'Standard Size' this scale is popular among model soldier collectors and is also known as 54mm. Airfix produce a small number of military models in this scale.

1/35

By far the most popular scale for military modelling. Tamiya started this particular ball rolling and chose 1/35 as it meant that they could fit an electric motor and a 'C' Type battery pack in a Panther tank; their first military model which was released in 1961. The scale grew in popularity in the 1970s and now totally dominates the market. New manufacturers in this scale regularly appear, particularly from the Far East and Eastern Europe. The vast array of kits of just about every vehicle and soldier that ever existed makes it a very attractive scale. Perhaps the only drawback is the space that completed models take up when compared to the smaller scales.

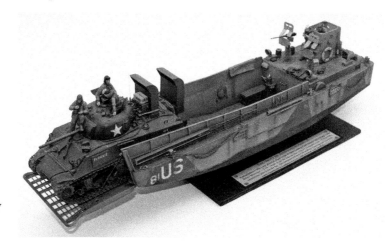

Although 1/35 scale is very detailed the models do take up more room than the smaller scales. This LCM 3 Landing Craft and Sherman by Simon Ward easily fills a shelf in a model-maker's display cabinet. (See the 1/72 equivalent above)

The 1/35 Sherman shown in the previous photograph showing the detailed crew. Model by Simon Ward.

1/24

Tamiya produced some tanks in this scale and there are specialist manufacturers like Kit Form Services that produce some highly detailed kits in this large scale.

1/16

Tamiya and Trumpeter produce military vehicles in this scale. Some are fully motorised but generally these kits are expensive (the Tamiya Panzer IV sells at around £500), so probably not the best choice if you are starting out in the hobby. For around £100 you can buy a remote control ready-to-run tank. Built for rugged handling, they are not as detailed as those from traditional kit manufacturers, but they are proving popular.

1/6

Those old enough will remember the 12-inch tall Action Man figures. They were 1/6 scale and, although you could buy a hard-plastic tank for these figures, the latest iteration in this scale is a million miles away from those toys of the 1960s. If you have a big budget or just want to make a once-in-a-lifetime purchase, then this might be the scale for you. Kits cost around £5,000 each and are fully motorised and remote controlled. Made from aluminium, brass and steel, assembly is relatively straight forward using household tools.

Pick Your Period

Once you have decided on your scale you will probably want to select a period to model and maybe a particular belligerent.

The First World War and the interwar period, 1916–1939.
There used to be very few models to represent early armour. The 100th anniversary of the First World War starting resulted in a veritable flood of new kits in both 1/72 and 1/35. Interwar tanks are still scarce from the major manufacturers, but in the smaller scale of 1/76 Geisbers Models produce a range of the more unusual AFVs of this era.

Second World War 1939–1945.
By far the most popular era, despite having the shortest span in terms of years. Most subjects are covered in the most popular scales of 1/72 and 1/35, and where there are gaps the small scale (in all senses) cottage industry producers like Milicast and Matador Models fill the gaps with resin models in 1/76. The majority of 1/48 scale kits are from vehicles of this era.

Modern, 1945–today.
You could subdivide the modern era into a Post-War Era (1945–1980s), and a Contemporary Era (1980s–today), based on the introduction of tanks like the Challenger, Abrams and Leopard 2 whose spaced armour gives them a very

Tanks first appeared in 1916. Models of these early AFVs are readily available in a variety of scales. The kit shown is from Master Box.

The Second World War has always been a popular period. The Churchill tank here is in Soviet service in winter colours.

The Soviet Josef Stalin IS 3 was a potent weapon when it first appeared in 1945. It was heavily modified with spaced armour fitted by the Iraqi Army to produce the IS3 Enigma. Model in 1/35 scale by Mark Gilbert.

Main battle tank chassis are often adapted by modern manufacturers to produce real life conversions. Using the Leopard chassis, the Gepard is a potent anti-aircraft weapon. Another splendid model in 1/35 scale from Mark Gilbert.

All nations that fought in the Second World War are represented in all of the popular scales, but British armour has been poorly represented, particularly in small scales. Here is a Revell Cromwell in 1/72 scale.

different look to anything that came before. In both sub-periods there are large numbers of injection moulded kits available to cover most of the post-Second World War subjects.

Decide on the Nation

Many modellers choose to model vehicles from a particular country. Second World War German tanks seem to have a mystical hold over the model making fraternity. All German tanks from the era are covered in virtually every version in the most popular scales. When the major manufacturers ran out of subjects some resorted to 'Paper Panzers' – vehicles that by the end of the Second World War existed either as drawings in the offices of bombed-out German tank factories in 1945, or else were no more than figments of imagination. For those of us that modelled Allied vehicles in small scale, we watched all these kits of German AFVs arrive while still without a decent Cromwell – the mainstay of British armour in the Second World War – until 2001 when Revell produced one.

Following a Theme

Some model makers select models based on a theme. It can be a specific period or one particular belligerent or even a single type of tank. The British Matilda tank was one of my favourites and I built several versions based on the Matilda II. Today the plethora of new kits means that the AFVs from most countries are available. Even nations like Poland that played only a short role in the war, or Japan who had only a few AFVs, are catered for in the most popular scales.

So, once you have decided on your scale, the era and the nation that you are modelling, you are all ready to go and make a purchase. Most model makers will follow the well-worn path of modern-day shoppers and go straight to the Internet and trawl around for the best deal. And why not? However, if you have a local model shop or a hobby shop that sells kits why not make that your first port of call? As I set out in Chapter 1, there was always a thrill of going to the local model shop and finding something you wanted. Even if I couldn't find exactly what I wanted, I seldom came away empty handed and this would set me off on a different track. With the kit, tools and paint bought you are now ready to embark on your next adventure! And that really is the point. Model making should be great fun. You may be disappointed with your early results, but as explained earlier it is a journey and one that may take some time and perhaps will never be completed. But buying that kit and all the associated things to build and paint it is just the first important step.

The Australians also used the Matilda as a bulldozer tank. This model is the Airfix Matilda fitted with a Matador Models bulldozer blade.

The Australian Army received many Matildas when they were judged to be obsolete for fighting in Africa and Europe, and one variant they used was armed with a flame thrower and called the Matilda Frog.

Although poorly armed compared to Soviet tanks, many Matildas went to the Eastern Front under Lend Lease. Airfix Matilda with Preiser figures.

For the attack on Bardia, in the Western Desert, a trench crossing Bailey Bridge was fitted to the front of a Matilda. The bridge section is from the Revell Churchill AVRE Bridge-layer kit.

There are some records of captured Matildas on the Eastern Front having their turrets removed and being used by the Germans as artillery tractors.

A real-life conversion was an experiment to fit an A24 Cavalier turret to a Matilda chassis. The reason for this is difficult to understand as it would require significant changes to the Matilda turret ring and the resulting tank would have little better armoured protection and be slower than the donor Cavalier tank. However, it does make an unusual model.

Practical Tips for Making Better Models

There can be no doubt that model making is an art form. Different model makers have their own styles and techniques and that is the cornerstone of your model making ability. However, having the right tools, and skills to use them, will help you produce the best models you possibly can.

Tools Essentials

If you are just starting out in the hobby or returning after a break and need some new tools here are my top tips.

1. Buy the best you can afford

Few things in the hobby are more frustrating than a blunt knife blade or pair of cutters that do not cut, or a paintbrush that sheds hairs like a moulting badger. Collecting a set of good tools does not have to be expensive. Here are the basics:

Craft knife/scalpel
Choose a knife that has changeable blades. I have two different Swann-Morton scalpel handles and use a variety of blades with each. Large blades shaped like a shark's fin are good for straight lines. Thinner more pointed blades are better for curves. A hook-like blade is really good for scrapping the inside of tubes or round edges. But whatever the job, the blade must be sharp. Blades are relatively cheap, so for each new project I fit a new blade to each handle.

Cutting mats
A good, firm work surface is essential, and a cutting mat can help ensure there are no gouges left on the dining room table after a modelling session. If you are going to cut plastic card, then a good 'self-healing' mat is essential. Readily available from art shops they provide protection for precious tables as well as cushioning the cutting action to help keep the blade sharp.

Cutters
A pair of special sprue cutters are really useful for cutting parts off the sprue. A pair of heavy cutters are essential for cutting large parts off a thick sprue, or for cutting

thick materials (resin or soft metal). Like craft knives, the sharper the better. Do not be tempted to twist a part off the sprue – you will invariably damage it.

Craft knives come in a variety of shapes and sizes.

A cutting mat is an essential item and readily available from craft and model shops.

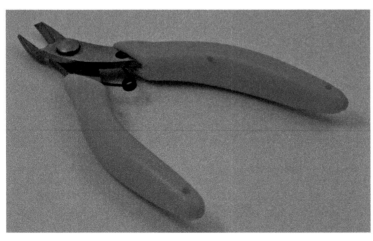

Special cutters like the ones shown are useful for cutting parts from the sprue.

Files and sanding sticks

Fine metal files give a good smooth finish and round files are good for expanding drilled holes. But keep them clean and do not be too vigorous when sanding as the heat generated can melt the plastic. Sanding sticks are abrasive strips like sandpaper fixed to a stiff but soft foam material. They are available in a variety of grades from coarse to ultra-smooth. Fine-grade wet and dry paper sheets are useful for cleaning metal parts.

Tweezers

Reverse action tweezers are the most useful as they clamp around the part and do not require the modeller to apply pressure to keep them closed. They are also useful for clamping small parts together while the glue dries.

Drills and drill bits

Fine drill bits can be held in a pin vice and larger drill bits twisted between finger and thumb. You only need a few different diameter bits. I have a set of seven bits from Dremel that have lasted for many, many models.

Sanding sticks are better to use on plastics than files.

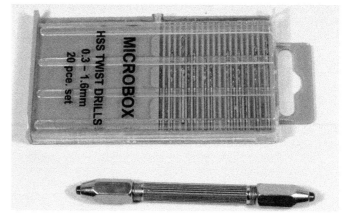

Drill bits for model makers are readily available and the ones shown are a useful range of sizes.

2. Use the right tool for the job

The tools above are the basics but as you become more skilled you will need to buy a few more tools. You can get by without them but using the right tool not only improves the result, it also enhances the whole experience:

Pliers
These are useful for bending metal parts to the required shape and for holding components firmly while you apply glue.

Clamps
If you are using a polystyrene glue it can, depending on the brand, take some time to set. Large assemblies can be held together while the glue dries and this could be achieved using something as simple as an elastic band wrapped around the two parts, or you could use a set of clamps. These can be quite cheap and readily available from DIY stores.

Razor saw
A fine-toothed blade is useful for cutting fine and delicate items off the sprue. While a craft knife can be used, the gentle cutting action of a fine-toothed saw will help ensure the item does not snap or ping off the sprue to end up lost in the carpet.

These cheap clamps are ideal for holding parts together while glue dries.

Razor saws can be used to cut large parts off a sprue.

Set square and metal ruler
If you move on to converting or scratch-building you will invariably use plastic card, and to make sure the parts you make are straight and true a good quality set square and metal ruler are essential.

Plastic scriber
A scriber is like a scalpel blade but, rather than cutting through a sheet, it cuts a groove and is ideal for making panel lines or depicting wooden slats.

Magnifying lenses
Styles and sizes are available varying from handheld to desk-mounted with an integral light surrounding the lens. I have recently started using some close-up lenses that can be worn like spectacles. While not great fashion accessories (don't wear them in public!) they are really useful as they magnify the subject yet leave hands free for holding and painting.

Micro chisel
Designed for the model maker, this chisel has a very narrow edge that is useful for getting in the places where it is difficult to remove surface detail.

Circle cutter
This cutter is adjustable so that circles of different diameters can be cut. These cutters can be used with very thin plastic card.

A set square can be used to ensure assemblies are square.

This scriber can be used to engrave panel lines in plastic sheet.

A really useful aid when assembling small parts are wearable lenses like those shown here.

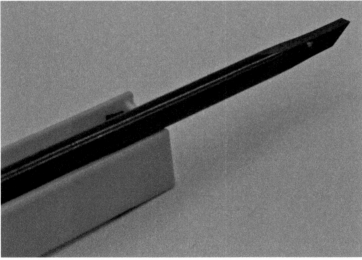

The narrow edge on this micro chisel makes it easy to get into places other tools cannot reach.

Callipers
These are useful if converting or scratch-building and you need to take measurements from a scale drawing. Once measured, you can mark plastic card to give you a measurement that is more accurate than using a ruler and pencil.

Photo etch jig
If you add detailing parts from photo-etched sets then a jig can be useful. They come in a variety of shapes and sizes. I tend to find flat-nose pliers and the edge of my set square are all I need. However, I don't use a lot of etched brass, I know some that do and find a jig essential.

Tacky wax has a number of uses when building kits as it provides a temporary bond.

Tacky Wax
If you want to put things together to see how they look then 'Tacky Wax' is the answer. This is really useful for working out the position of arms, legs and heads on figures.

3. Use the right glue

When I first started building kits polystyrene cement came in metal tubes (lead!) and epoxy resins provided a strong bond but took hours to set. There were various general-purpose glues available, but they were only useful for card and paper, and that was about it. Today there seems to be a special glue for every requirement. The list below outlines some that are available:

Polystyrene cement
This glue works by melting the plastic to fuse it together. So, while good for sticking together large components other glues are better for small parts. But for sticking plastic to plastic this is probably the best glue to use. It is now available in a variety of dispensers. Using traditional tube glue is always a bit of a gamble as squeezing too hard can flood the parts you are trying to cement together. Most 'poly' glue is sold in semi-rigid plastic bottles that dispense the glue in drops via a fairly coarse hollow needle. Glass bottles of glue often come with an integral brush that you can use to apply the glue. However, this can lead to too much glue being applied, so I dip a cocktail stick into the bottle to apply a small amount of glue. It is always better to apply too little glue than too much. When gluing together two large parts I put the parts together dry and then run some cement along the join and allow capillary action to make the glue flow between the parts.

Super glue
Cyanoacrylate adhesives is the technical name for what is more commonly known as super glue. These glues have been available since the late 1970s but became widely used from the 1980s, from a variety of manufacturers. There are numerous types available and the means of dispensing is the main factor in deciding which glue is best for the model maker. The glues most suitable for model makers take a short time to

set so that you can position the part before the glue sets. Some glues are instant setting and are good for fitting tiny parts when you are confident that you can put them in exactly the right place. If you do get it wrong, then do not try to apply more super glue to super glue that has already set. You need to rub off the set glue and start again. The application of superglue can be a challenge. I have a set of specialist applicators that overcome most of the problems.

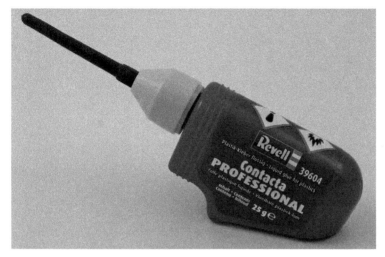

Polystyrene glue is best glue to use when assembling plastic kits.

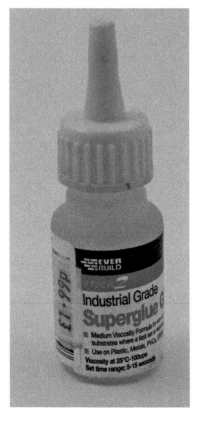

Cyanoacrylate adhesives has a trade name of 'Superglue' and is very useful for sticking small parts.

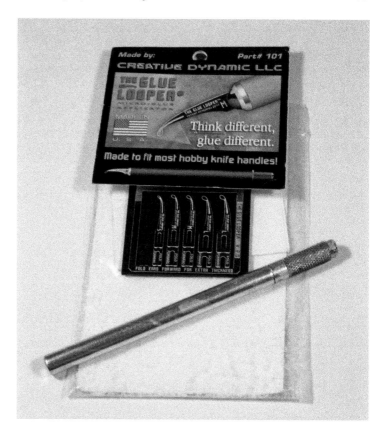

Only a small amount of super glue is normally needed, and the tools shown are useful for the application of this type of glue.

The Gorilla range of glues have numerous applications.

Specialist glues

Epoxy resins are provided as two separate tubes: one containing the adhesive and the second the hardener. Once thoroughly mixed the glue starts to set and setting times can vary. For model makers the 'five minute' epoxy is the most suitable for most applications. Other glues need water to activate them. Some glues have specialist uses such as metal bonding.

Miliput is useful for filling holes and gaps in an assembled model.

Glue for soft plastic
Most small-scale figures are made of a soft polythene type plastic that can bend without breaking (Airfix soldiers are typical). Normal plastic cement will not hold soft plastic parts together, so for this application 'Soft Plastic' from Glu & Fix is one of the best glues to use.

General purpose glues
Other good general-purpose adhesives are ideal for scenery building. White PVA glue is a thin version of this glue that is good for coating soft plastic soldiers to provide a firm undercoat for painting.

Fillers
In small-scale modelling it is worth having some filler to hand for conversions or scratch-building. Fillers can come as two chemicals that you combine such as Milliput Fine, or as a tube of filler such as Deluxe Materials Perfect Plastic Putty.

4. Be patient

Model making certainly teaches patience. I now find that the more kits I build the longer it takes to build each one. This is mainly because I invariably make a few modifications and add extra detailing. Building 'Out of the Box' is no longer an option! For suspension assemblies it is essential to let the glue set, as putting the tracks around road wheels shortly after attaching the wheels to the chassis will inevitably lead to warped and unrealistic suspension. Leaving a model overnight for the suspension to set hard is often a good idea.

5. Build up a good spares box

Many modern kits come with optional parts and these unused parts should be kept to one side as they may come in useful if you want to detail, convert or scratch-build models in the future. Some pieces of sprue are worth keeping as they can be cut, filed or stretched to make new parts.

There are numerous clubs and societies both in the UK and internationally. Members of the Miniature Armoured Fighting Vehicle Association are shown here enjoying a day out.

6. Join a club

Model making is a solitary occupation but a visit to a local model show will both inspire you and enable you to talk to like-minded people about your favourite hobby. The International Plastic Modelling Society (IPMS) and Miniature Armoured Fighting Vehicle Association (MAFVA) hold regular meetings throughout Britain (and indeed worldwide). The members of IPMS and MAFVA have a wealth of experience and information and many have the confidence and skill to share their knowledge with you. If you have a local model shop they will probably have details of a nearby model club or if you attend a model show then doubtless there will be several local clubs that will be pleased to see you as a new member. Some military modelling magazines have a calendar of up-and-coming model making shows and it is worth a look to see what is available in your area.

7. Keep building!

If you are new to the hobby you may be disappointed by your first efforts. However, you will find that practice leads to raising your standards and the more you build the better the results. Military model making in the small scales does not have to be an expensive hobby, so if you do totally ruin a model it can be consigned to the bin. However, the chances are that if you put it to one side there will come a time when you can re-visit that particular model and rescue it or make it into a battle-damaged casualty.

Detailing Your Models

When I first started building kits in the 1970s it was for the wargames table. They had to be robust and suitable for rough handling as well as regular moves from battlefield to battlefield, often in a cardboard box with little padding. When I moved from wargamer to collector the needs changed. Hatches were opened with crew figures installed in realistic poses; antennas sprouted from turrets and anti-aircraft machine guns fitted on delicate mountings. Real tanks are not just fighting machines, they are home to the crew and, with inside space limited, most tank rear hulls would become festooned with 'kit'. Modern models come complete with detailed parts and some with stowage. But failing that, items like additional tools, fuel cans (known as Jerry cans), towing cables and rolled up tarpaulins and camouflage netting can be bought from after-market suppliers, or you can make them from scratch.

Model kits in the early days were often simplified and lacking detail. Even modern kits can be improved by the addition of parts from various after-market suppliers. It only takes a little work to add extra detail. Because they are delicate-looking it is

Some major manufacturers are now making wargaming tanks. Simple to construct they do lack the detail that model collectors demand. Here a 1/72 T34/85 designed for wargamers has hatches opened and crew figures added. (Photograph by Alex Cossey)

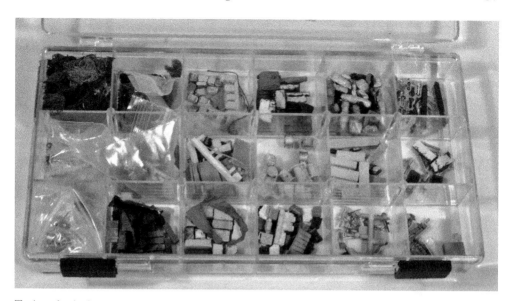

Tools and vehicle stowage can be bought separately or homemade. Here are a selection from a number of suppliers in 1/72 scale.

Small-scale tracks were often the least realistic part of the kit. Often described as 'rubber band tracks', more modern kits have much more detailed tracks provided in hard plastic as link and length, as shown with these kit tracks for the Revell Cromwell.

Small-scale tracks are also available as etched brass. They do require accurate bending to make something that looks acceptable.

difficult for a kit manufacturer to accurately replicate grab handles. But they are very easy to reproduce using thin brass wire. Plastic headlamps can be replaced by more realistic-looking glass lenses that are readily available. The tracks provided in many kits – particularly in the small scales – often lack detail and do not sit properly on the suspension. Some modern kits have dispensed with the old 'rubber bands' and some kits are provided with individual links and others are available as etched brass.

In recent years there has been a growth in etched brass detailing kits. In small scale these parts can be tiny and almost impossible to fit. The difficulty with the really small components (apart from actually seeing them) is fixing them to the kit. Superglue can be used but often the part is so small that only a tiny amount of glue can be applied, and even if the part does adhere to the kit it will almost inevitably fly off when you apply some paint. However, there are some good detailing parts around that do help to improve the overall look of the kit. One easy thing to do is replace the gun barrel. Plastic kit parts are moulded as two parts and it is difficult to get a round barrel if you have to sand down a seam. Although not cheap, metal gun barrels and muzzle brakes can make a big improvement to the look of your model.

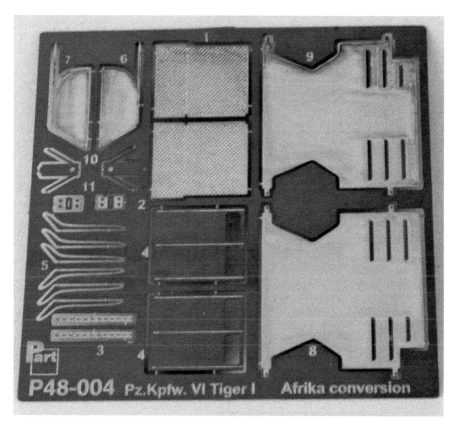

Etched brass provides some additional parts to add extra detail to your model. Mainly available in 1/35 scale, detailing kits for smaller scales, like this set for 1/48 Tiger, are becoming more readily available.

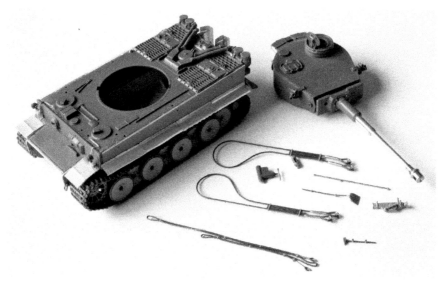

Tamiya 1/48 scale Tiger with etched brass track guards and exhaust covers fitted as well as a turned metal barrel. Wire handles can be seen on the turret hatches.

The headlamps on some early Tigers were moved from the top of the hull to stop them being knocked off by the main gun. Kit headlamps fitted into etched brass and resin holders with cable made from a piece of wire.

Etched brass track guards seen close up. Photographs of the real thing show they were easily bent and twisted. The kit provides a single thick plastic part that does not look right.

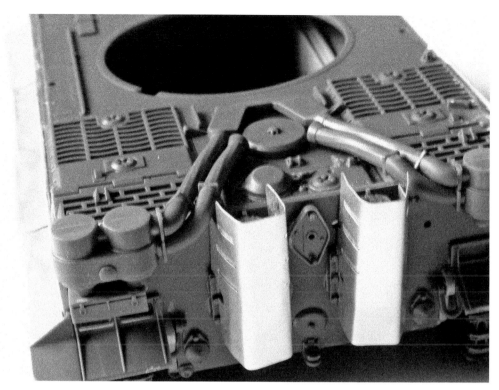

The exhaust covers on the Tiger tank were flimsy and these etched brass replacements are a better scale thickness than the plastic parts provided.

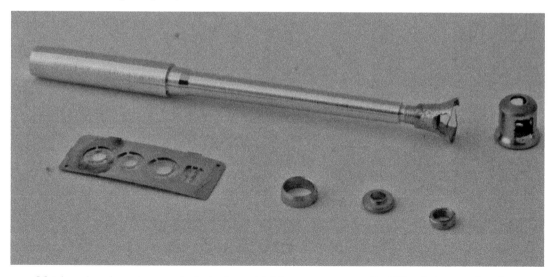

Metal gun barrels can improve the look of a model. Most guns are covered in 1/35 scale but more barrels in 1/72 and 1/48 are becoming available.

When I first began model making there were only a few small-scale AFV kits available. New releases from Airfix were greeted with much excitement, with announcements in modelling magazines months before the kits were released. The arrival of the Matchbox range of kits in late 1970s gave a significant boost to all those modelling in 1/76 scale. However, there were still significant gaps and the model makers in the 1970s and 1980s had to resort to scratch-building with plastic card or convert existing kits to fill these gaps. Books in the Airfix Magazine range were inspiring. Today the range of small-scale kits (particularly in 1/72 scale) is so vast that almost every subject is now covered. Even if the main injection moulding manufacturers do not yet produce a model of a particular vehicle, chances are that it is covered by one of the 'cottage industry' resin manufacturers (such as Milicast, Geisbers and Friendship Models). If the subject is still not covered you may be able to find a suitable aftermarket conversion kit from a variety of small manufacturers (like Matador Models). I still occasionally convert small scale models but as is the case with the Crusader AA shown, IBG released a kit of the same vehicle shortly after I completed the conversion.

So why scratch-build or even convert? Like all art forms (and model making can be seen as an art form) building military vehicles offers an opportunity for artistic expression. With a modicum of knowledge and practice most people will be able to put together a plastic kit

Airfix Magazine Guides provided model makers in the 1970s and 1980s with useful scale drawings.

Crusader III AA Mk I converted from a Hasagawa Crusader with a 40 mm Bofors from Zvezda. IGB have announced they are to release a kit of this AFV shortly after this conversion was built. (Photograph by Alex Cossey)

straight out of the box. Some model makers will be content to put together a kit with few or no changes or modifications. Others will feel the need to address the manufacturer's errors or may wish to build a different version to the one in the box. The next level is to convert a model into something based on the kit but with major changes. The final level is to build something totally from scratch. Not all modellers will pass through all those levels. There are few model makers that scratch-build these days but converting and detailing a kit enables the model maker to produce something new and unique.

If you decide to convert or scratch-build, the materials required are readily available from hobby and model shops. Plastic card (also known as the trade name Plastikard) is the main material for scratch-building and converting. High Impact Polystyrene Sheet comes in sheets that measure 9' x 12' (nominally 220 mm x 330 mm) in a variety of thicknesses. Normally measured in thousandths of an inch (Thou) the sheets are normally white, but some sizes can be found in black and clear.

As well as plastic sheets modellers can use plastic rods and tubes in a variety of shapes such as channels and 'H' beams. These can be cut to produce small details like grab handles. Some model makers use other materials like wood (soft wood like balsa being easiest to shape).

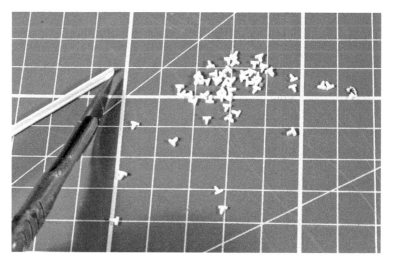

Slicing the end of a plastic T-shaped girder yields up some useful shapes. These parts became the teeth for some scratch-built tracks for a 1/76 scale Grant tank.

Painting and Finishing Your Model

While building the model is essential, it is at the painting stage that the model maker applies their stamp of individuality. Most people can put together a construction kit, but it is in the painting and weathering stage that the true artistic flair emerges. As your skills develop so you should see the results improve. Like many things experience through practice helps and the following pages contain tips and advice built up over many years.

Applying the Paint

There are three ways to apply the paint to your model. Let's look at each in detail.

Paintbrush
Most model makers will start off with a hand-held paintbrush. Many will stay with the brush and there is nothing wrong with this. The main rule to follow is to buy the best brush you can. Most cheap brushes shed hairs like a moulting badger and don't last long. I use Windsor and Newton Series 7 brushes for fine detail. They are not cheap at £10 a brush but they do retain a fine tip and, as long as you look after them, will last for a long time. On the subject of care, if you have invested a lot of money in a brush it makes sense to look after it. Once you have finished painting a shade clean thoroughly with a suitable solvent and dry off with kitchen roll or tissue. At the end of your painting session take the time to give all the brushes you have used a deep clean. I use a brand of 'brush restorer' to get all the paint off the brush and then rinse in warm soapy water with a final rinse in cold water. Because acrylic paint dries quickly there is a danger that dried paint will build up in the root of the hairs, so a thorough clean is essential.

Spray can
There is a large range of spray paint for the modeller now available. While the range is not as extensive as pots of paint, several major manufacturers (Humbrol and Tamiya to name but two) produce shades for the model maker in spray cans. I use spray cans to prime my models either in black or grey. I have used spray cans sold for car repairs as an undercoat, but they do go on thickly and obscure the detail, so it is preferable to use a spray paint that is designed for model makers. There are three issues with spray cans. As stated, it is easy to spray too much paint on and this obscures detail. The second issue is the limited range of colours available. Thirdly, the spray cannot be adjusted so it's not possible to paint convincing camouflage schemes like you can with

an airbrush. However, if you are painting lots of models in single standard colours, spray cans have a lot to recommend them.

Airbrush
Undoubtedly the best way to apply paint to a model is via an airbrush. Airbrushing delivers a thin layer paint and is essential for numerous applications such as feather edge camouflage schemes and weathering. However, airbrushes and associated compressors are not cheap. A good quality airbrush is around £100 and a suitable compressor costs around £200. You can buy a 'starter set' of a cheap airbrush and a can of compressed air for around £30. Although this is a good way to start (and I used this set up when I first started model making), the cheaper airbrushes have a limited use and the compressed air cans don't keep a constant pressure and invariably run out in the middle of a painting session. If you have the funds a good airbrush and compressor will make a big difference to the standard of your finished models.

Brushes can vary in price and normally the more expensive ones will hold their point longer and last but take great care to thoroughly clean after every use.

An airbrush compressor will probably be the most expensive piece of equipment most model makers will ever buy. An alternative is to use compressed air but the pressure out of these will vary as the can cools.

Types of paint

When I first started painting model kits only enamel paints from a small number of manufacturers were readily available. Today, not only is the range of available shades vast compared to the 1970s, but there is a choice between enamel and acrylic paints. Both have advantages and disadvantages as below.

Acrylics have two advantages: they dry quickly and, being water-based, cleaning brushes and airbrushes is simple, odourless and inexpensive. Because the paint dries quickly you can apply several layers in a modelling session, which is ideal for applying multiple colour camouflage schemes and for figure painting. Ironically fast drying is also a disadvantage as it means that airbrushes clog quickly, so if you are using acrylics in an airbrush you will need to regularly clean the brush during a painting session if you are spraying for a long time. Normal paint brushes need to be thoroughly cleaned too as the acrylic paint quickly dries and builds up in the roots of the brush. For figure painting I use Vallejo acrylics.

Enamel paints dry more slowly than acrylics but give better coverage and better definition when spraying camouflage patterns. Their disadvantage is that you have to wait for the enamel paint to dry before applying a second and third coat. The decision about which type of paint to use is very subjective. It's all a matter of your experiences and preferences. I tend to spray Humbrol enamels and Tamiya Xtra Colour acrylics.

Painting the model

Once you have decided on the paint and how you are going to apply it then it is time to get painting. The most important thing to remember is it is much better to apply several thin layers rather than one thick one. A thick layer of paint obscures detail and makes it difficult to apply the weathering techniques outlined later in this book.

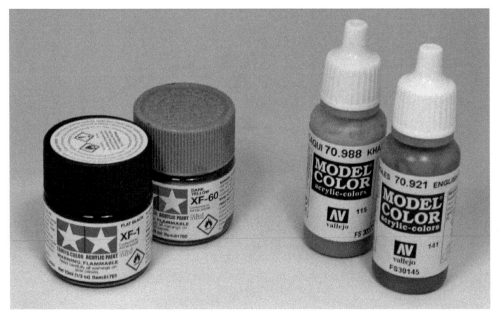

Arylic paints have been gaining in popularity over the past few years. They dry quickly and brushes can be washed in water.

The first layer to apply is the undercoat. This can be grey or black. I use black for vehicles that will be end up green and grey for lighter shades such as shades of desert sand or yellow. Humbrol produce a grey primer and matt black and these are ideal for applying the undercoat. Whenever using a spray can a light touch is essential to avoid putting on too much paint.

The second layer is the base coat. This is the colour that is the 'factory fresh' shade and is applied as one or two thin coats over the undercoat. If the undercoat shows through in places don't worry as there is more to add yet. The basecoat can be used

A primer undercoat gives an even colour for the next coats to cover. Black is used here on this 1/72 scale Grant.

This heavily converted Airfix Churchill has been primed in grey.

Base coat applied to a Cromwell. The stands are made from balsa wood and a milk container cap. These stands make handling easier when painting.

straight from the bottle or can. To take account of the 'scale effect' some will lighten this shade by adding around 15 per cent white, or a suitable light colour like yellow if you are applying green.

With the base coat applied the model looks flat and toy like. In the real world light hits the upper surface of a vehicle and scatters evenly, lower surfaces can be in the shade and so can sometimes look a different shade (take a look at a car that is a 'solid' colour in bright sunlight to see this effect). A small-scale model does not exhibit the same properties and so, to simulate this, spray the model again with the basecoat colour to which white or a lighter colour has been added. Spray the top of the model only so that the upper surfaces are lighter in colour. If using a paintbrush, you can apply a dot of paint (I use oil paint that is a lighter shade of the base colour) in the middle of an upper surface panel and then drag the paint using a dry brush from the centre of the panel to the edges. You may wish to use this technique even if you have already sprayed the model with the lighter shade from above. The effect has to be subtle and the aim is to break up the solid colour of the base coat.

With the shading complete the model should look more life-like. If applicable, it is now time to apply the camouflage scheme. Allied vehicles, particularly those that were used in the second half of Second World War seldom carried camouflage schemes and appeared mainly in Olive Drab. Axis vehicles, particularly late-war German vehicles, used three colour 'ambush' patterns. Hard edged schemes can be applied with a paintbrush. If using an airbrush, mask off the areas of the base colour that you want to stay that colour. The mask can be masking tape or a soft putty like Blu-Tack. Soft edge camouflage patterns need to be applied by an airbrush. Whether hard or soft edged, the camouflage patterns need to be toned down by either over-spraying a thin layer of the base colour across the whole model, or by dry brushing the model with the base colour.

Oil-based enamel paints will not mix with water-based acrylics. When it comes to diluting paint, in my experience it is best to use the thinners provided by the paint manufacturer (so use Humbrol thinners with Humbrol paint). The composition of paint varies between manufacturers, so if you are mixing paints to produce a new shade or make the shade lighter or darker it is best to mix together paints from the same manufacturer. Using turpentine for enamels and water for acrylics to clean paint brushes and air brushes is not a problem.

Once the painting stages are complete and you are happy with the overall appearance it is time to leave the paint to dry. The time taken varies depending on whether you are using oil-based enamels or acrylics. However, regardless of paint type I tend to leave the model overnight to thoroughly dry.

Painting a hard edge camouflage scheme using Blu-Tac and an airbrush.

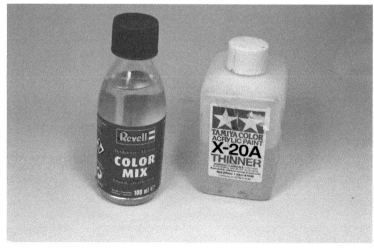

Paints from different manufacturers vary in composition. Using the thinners from the same manufacturer as the paint normally produces the best results.

Varnish and Decals

The next stage is to seal the model. This provides a protective barrier for the weathering stage and also tones the colours down to give a better finish. You can seal the model using proprietary varnishes (matt rather than gloss) and these can be applied using a brush or spray can or an airbrush as per the painting stages. I use an acrylic floor sealant called Klear. This is very thin and can be easily sprayed on the model or alternatively can be applied with a wide paintbrush. It dries quickly and produces a semi-matt appearance.

The next stage is to apply the decals (also known as transfers). Most kits come with a set of decals that normally represent the markings of a particular vehicle. Some kits will have sufficient decals to enable you to model several different vehicles. If you need to represent a vehicle not covered in the kit, there are a vast number of companies that produce numerous sheets of decals covering many subjects.

The majority of decals are known as waterslide because they are applied by dipping them in warm water. Once the decal starts to become loose remove from the water and slide the decal onto the model. I wet the surface where the decal is going to be applied with a decal solution like Micro-sol. This softens the decal on contact, and this will help you mould the decal to the contours on the vehicle. I usually gently press the decal down with a piece of kitchen roll or tissue but leave the decal slightly wet so that it dries through evaporation. Leave for a short while so that the decal can set and then press down on the decal with a tissue to absorb any moisture. Once dry, spray with a matt varnish to protect the decal from the weathering stage and fix the decal in place.

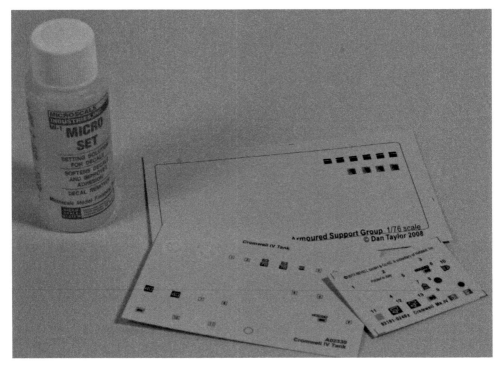

Using a decal softener ensures the decal better follows the contours of your model making it look more realistic.

Weathering Washes

While the construction and painting phases provide the foundation for a good model, the weathering stage can make a model that was average look outstanding. The techniques in this section are a basic guide. There are many books and many more articles on the internet that cover the subject in much greater depth but hopefully this section will give a good foundation to those new to the hobby, and a few pointers for those who are not so new.

Weathering can involve coating the model with paints and washes that can react with the paint on the model causing the underlying coats, so carefully applied, to run and thereby ruining the overall finish. So, it is always important to apply a barrier layer between your painted model and the weathering layers. I use Klear; it is easy to apply, goes on thinly and gives the model a metallic sheen. You can use matt, satin or gloss varnish that can be applied by brush, airbrush or from an aerosol. The most important thing to remember is that each layer reduces the level of detail so apply thinly but evenly over your precious model.

A wash (a very thin wash is sometimes known as a filter) is very thin paint that flows into the niches and recesses and brings out the detail like no other process. A great variety of washes are available ready mixed, or you can make your own. Commercial washes come in a variety of mediums, shades and colours. It's a part of the hobby that has grown exponentially over the past few years with washes and filters now produced by a variety of manufacturers. There are a few that I like and use but that is the result of some years of experimenting. I normally make my own by adding a small amount of Burnt Umber oil paint to thinners in the ratio of 10 per cent oil paint to 90 per cent thinners. This is applied using a soft wide brush over the whole model.

Applying washes takes practice. If you use too much wash the panel lines will fill with the paint and overflow with pooling at some points. It is essential to remove the excess, and if there is a lot of excess dab this off with a piece of kitchen roll before the

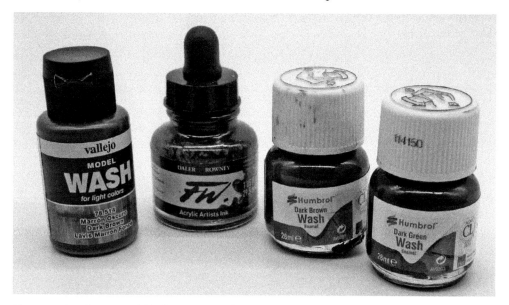

Commercial washes are available from a variety of sources.

wash dries. If there is only a small amount of excess then a broad, chisel shaped brush dipped in a small amount of thinners can be used to remove the excess. However, if it all goes horribly wrong and there is too much wash then you can rinse the wash off with thinners and start again (it is essential to let the model completely dry before trying again).

A second type of wash is more subtle and uses a thin, pointed brush to pick out individual details by applying a tiny amount of wash next to a prominent feature, such as a rivet head or hatch detail. This is known as a pin wash. The wash flows around the object giving it a false shadow that makes it look more prominent. The pin wash can also be used to emphasise panel lines. With the right mix the paint flows along the panel lines and around prominent objects through capillary action. Pin washes can be used to supplement the overall wash or just used alone.

As well as bringing out the fine detail on a vehicle, washes can be used to depict the effect of weather on a vehicle. Rain streaks can be produced by running some heavily diluted

A 1/48 Scale Tiger I as used in Tunisia showing details emphasised by a pin wash around the mantlet. (Photograph by Alex Cossey)

Rain streaks can be applied by running very diluted washes down vertical surfaces.

(10 per cent paint to 90 per cent thinners) buff-coloured oil paint, with a wide soft brush, from the upper surfaces of the vehicle slowly downwards in the direction that rain would flow. Once you are content with the wash the model is set aside to dry, preferably overnight.

Dust

We are surrounded by real life weathering (although this involves dust and grime rather than washes!). If you leave your car unwashed for several weeks you will find an even build-up of dust in the summer and grime in the winter over your car (I leave mine unwashed for six months at a time so I can study thiseffect …). Real tanks acquire this dust and grime depending on where they are operating, and so model makers look to replicate this. You can buy purpose-made dust from a variety of manufacturers in a variety of colours. 'Europe Dust' from MIG and 'European Earth' from AK Pigments are typical of those available. You could make your own dust by using an appropriate shade of chalk pastel that is rubbed along a piece of sandpaper. Whichever you choose the dust is then applied with a soft brush around tracks, running gear and on flat upper surfaces. If the model is being placed in a diorama or will not be handled, then you can finish at this point. If you want to make the dust a more permanent fixture, then you need to spray the model with matt varnish. Unfortunately, spraying the dust makes it take on a more prominent and unrealistic appearance. The other way to replicate dust is to spray an appropriate colour onto the running gear and tracks. The effect is subtle as a single pass with the airbrush set to low pressure should be enough the replicate a thin layer of dust.

Mud

While dust is prevalent in summer, the onset of winter will turn non-metalled roads into muddy trails and tracks are a most effective means of churning up this mud. As with model dust there are a number of companies that produce model mud. You can make your own mud using pigments or chalk pastels of the appropriate colour, to which a small amount of varnish and thinners are added. Whether commercial or homemade, the mud can be applied around running gear, tracks and spread onto the lower hull. There is a danger here of applying mud too thickly. In real life, tracks and suspension units are designed to throw off the mud as this can clog up suspension units and tracks causing them to fail. Crews, therefore, would clean off the mud whenever time and the situation allowed.

Chips and Wear

The final stage in the weathering process is to add some chips to the paint work and depict the wear and tear that results from the crew climbing over the vehicle. A soft graphite pencil (2B) with a sharp tip can be used to represent small paint chips. Look at a real vehicle and you will see these are most prevalent in areas where the crew clamber in and out of the vehicle, and so should be mainly around the hatches. This is another effect that is easy to overdo, so it is best to add a few chips at a time and then take a good look at the model before adding too many and spoiling the overall effect.

1/35 scale **M32** Recovery Tank from Simon Ward showing tracks and suspension units lightly coated with mud.

1/72 scale Grant tank lightly dusted to reflect desert conditions. (Photograph by Alex Cossey)

Summary

There can be no doubt that the painting and weathering stages are the most artistic phase of the model making process. The techniques above are not exhaustive and new techniques are being developed all the time but as you learn you will develop your own style. One thing I would urge though is to base your techniques on real vehicles and not base them on the work of other modellers. The modelling press (both in magazines and online) is full of articles that show the best way to paint and finish a model. Many are stunning and inspiring but slavishly following others' techniques could well stifle your own skills. Perfection is subjective and one set of techniques applicable to one finish may not be applicable to a different finish. As with many things it takes practice, but perhaps the greatest joy is you can continually learn and develop your skills and enjoy the fruits of your labours as your models improve with this practice.

First World War
and the Interwar Period

In 1916 the face of land warfare would change for ever. The first armoured vehicles crawled towards the German lines and had virtually no impact on the First World War at this time. The early tanks were experimental and dismissed by the Germans and some Allied generals as nothing more than a novel toy. The Battle of Cambria in November 1917 would change all that when tanks were used for the first time en masse and across ground that had not been churned up by a heavy artillery bombardment before the attack. The British and French Allies used tanks to great effect after Cambria. Although the Germans pressed some captured tanks into service, they built only around twenty of their own.

First World War Tanks from Mother to Mk III

Until recently there were very few models in any scale available of First World War tanks. Airfix first released the kit they called 'World War I Tank' in 1967 when information was sparse compared with today. David Fletcher from the Bovington Tank Museum relates that the Airfix Mark I was modelled on the Mark II at the

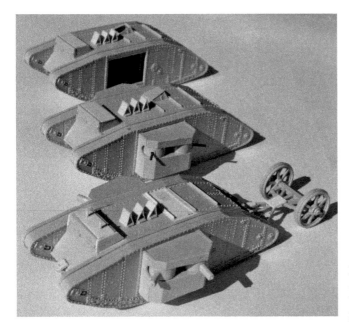

Production line of Mk I tanks. All based on the Airfix kits with the changes incorporated using plastic card.

Tank Museum, which was then known as HMLS *Dragonfly*. At the time the tank had been altered to become a Mark I, complete with tail wheels, an original male sponson on the left and a female sponson on the right. However, HMLS *Dragonfly* had been modified to serve as a supply tank and so was not even a good basis for a Mk II. Despite these inaccuracies, the Airfix WW1 tank makes a good foundation for all versions of the British First World War tank from the prototype, Mother, through to the Mark III. The table on page 59 shows the differences. In recent years the Airfix kits have been eclipsed by the kits from Masterbox. Linked to the anniversaries of the First World War, Masterbox released a number of kits of Mk I tanks in a variety of guises.

Based on the Airfix kit and depicted as the prototype 'Mother'.

An Airfix Mk I Female finished with figures from WD Models.

Mk III Female 'Somewhere in England.' Again from Airfix, with the small sponsons and access doors underneath.

Mk III Female with Vickers machine guns.

For many years the only small-scale First World War tank available was the aged Airfix tank. Today companies like Ehmar and Masterbox have a large range of tanks from the First World War in small scale.

	Mother	Mk I	Mk II	Mk III
Number built	One	75 Male 75 Female	25 Male 25 Female	25 Male 25 Female
Identification Numbers	N/A	701–775 – Male 501–575 – Female	776–800 Male 576–600 Female	801–825 Male 601–625 Female
Main Armament	2 x 6Pdr 40 calibre	Male-2 x 6Pdr 40 calibre Female-4 x Water cooled Vickers MG	Male-2 x 6Pdr 40 calibre Female-4 x Water cooled Vickers MG	Male-2 x 6Pdr 40 calibre Female-4 x Water cooled Lewis MG
Secondary Armament	None	Male: 3 x Lewis MG fired through apertures in front and each sponson.	Male: 3 x Lewis MG fired through apertures in front and each sponson.	Male: 3 x Lewis MG fired through apertures in front and each sponson.
Differences to previous Mk.	Not applicable	Additional springs added to tail. Perforations in hull plates above radiator eliminated. Inverted V baffle over exhaust outlets. Rivet spacing wider. Majority fitted with anti-grenade mesh over roof in France	Cab narrower by around 6 inches. Some tracks with 'spuds' fitted every sixth track link. Track adjustment increased by 1.5'(38 mm)so apertures on front horns different. Wedge shaped turret replaces manhole hatch. Steering tail removed. Hydraulic jack removed.	Some Female sponsons smaller than Mk II ones. Circular orifice in the front turret to hold a ball mounted Lewis gun. Front vision slits higher than in previous versions. Plate thicker than on previous versions but not hardened.
Use	Original trials held in Lincoln and Hatfield	First saw action on the Somme in 1916. A few used as supply tanks and some Females converted to wireless tanks in 1917.	Built to be used for training so constructed from un-armoured plate. Some tanks sent to France to take part in the Battle for Arras April 1917. Some converted to supply tanks.	Constructed from un-armoured plate and used for training only. Mainly used at Bovington.

(Continued)

	Mother	Mk I	Mk II	Mk III
Painting scheme	Admiralty grey with white undersides and between front track horns.	In England multi-colour scheme of green, yellow, brown and pink. Once in France toned down to green, brown and ochre with black disruptive lines.	Overall khaki brown. Some Females were fitted with MKI sponsons that retained their original camouflage pattern.	Overall khaki brown.

Mark IV and Beyond

Although Mother and the early marks of tank have their place in history, the use of the Mk IV tank at Cambrai marked the true start of armoured warfare. Ehmar have brought out a number of First World War tanks including a reasonable Mk IV (although marketed as 1/72 scale it is much nearer to 1/76). They also produce a Whippet tank and the German A7V.

HMLS Excellent was a Mk IV tank that was a Royal Navy gate guardian in Portsmouth. At the start of the Second World War, the AFV was refurbished with plans put in place to repulse a German invasion. Fortunately, it was never put to the test.

The Germans regarded the British tanks in the First World War as a novelty and put little effort in developing their own. The A7V was built in small numbers and a replica is seen here with A7V expert Max Hundleby in the foreground.

The Interwar Period

For many years the period between 1918 and 1939 was largely ignored by model kit manufacturers. But small-scale manufacturer Geisbers have tapped a rich source of subjects from this era and have produced some fine models in 1/76 scale. In 1/72 scale, Dragon have produced an early Panzer in the shape of the Neaubaufahrzeug Number 1. In 1/35 scale, Meng have also realised that there is a rich vein of unusual AFVs and have released a Vickers Medium in the larger scale as well as a Char D. The Vickers chassis was used as an artillery tractor at the start of the Second World War. But at a time when most subjects from the First and Second World War, and to a great extent post-1945, have been covered in all scales, the interwar period remains almost undiscovered by model kit manufacturers. It was a time of great experimentation by all the major nations and although many of the multi-turreted monsters progressed no further than a single prototype, this period was an important one for tank development. Perhaps in the next few years as manufacturers struggle to find something new, we will see more kits from this period.

The period between the wars was one of experimentation. One of the early Panzers built by the Germans was the Neubaufahrzeug Number 1, seen here in 1/72 scale from Dragon. (Photograph by Alex Cossey)

Hobby Boss Vickers Medium Tank in 1/35 scale is one of the few large-scale interwar period tanks available.

Meng produce a 1/35 scale Char 2C. (Photograph courtesy of Gary Wenko)

The interwar period is best served by small cottage industry manufacturers. This Dragon artillery tractor used by the BEF in 1939 is based on the Vickers Medium tank.

Netherlands-based Giesbers Models have a good range of interwar AFVs including the multi-turreted Independent.

'The Old Gang' was the name adopted by a group of designers who determined, in the 1930s, that the next war would need trench-crossing giant tanks and so designed and built TOG. Another from Giesbers Models in 1/76 scale.

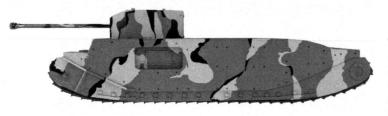

TOG still exists and is housed in the RAC Tank Museum at Bovington. It carries an interesting scheme that is shown here. (Drawing by Oliver Cole)

Second World War – British Armoured Vehicles

There has been a vast growth in the number of kit manufacturers and the number of new kits in all scales over the past few years. Going back to the 1970s it would have been possible to list all of the kits of military vehicles in a couple of pages. Today the list would probably fill several books this size, and it would be out of date in a few weeks as new model kits appear on an almost daily basis. Take a look at the competition table in most model shows, and the majority of vehicles will relate to the Second World War. This period of a little over six years has always been popular with model makers and manufacturers and the Second World War is a national obsession for the British. Many of us were brought up on films like *The Battle of Britain* and *The Great Escape* with *Dad's Army* and *'Allo 'Allo* flooding the living room once a week. Little wonder the Second World War is a popular period.

So, this chapter on British AFVs and the following chapter on German vehicles will only touch the tip of this model making iceberg. They will give a concise outline of some of the AFVs that were in service, with a limited outline of kits that are available, followed by a show case that concentrates on a single vehicle type in a few scales.

Early British Armour

Britain entered the Second World War with an army that had been starved of funding and was geared more around colonial policing than fighting a continental war. The British Expeditionary Force that landed in France within weeks of war being declared had some lightly armed and armoured light tanks and medium 'Cruisers', as well as some heavily armoured but lightly armed 'infantry' tanks. Although Britain had, in the 1920s and 1930s, laid the foundation for an all-arms force, it would be the Germans that would exploit this idea with devastating effect as the Panzers rolled through Poland, the Low Countries and France using 'blitzkrieg' tactics. There is still a paucity of models of BEF tanks in most scales. The gap left by the major manufacturers is filled by 'cottage industry' firms like Milicast, 1st Company and Bull Models. The early battles in the Western Desert were fought by the British using similar infantry and cruiser tanks and again examples are available from the smaller manufacturers.

The Matilda I was thickly armoured but had very vulnerable tracks and only a machine gun as the main armament. This superb 1/48 scale model is from 1st Company.

Despite the name, Matilda II was not a development of Matilda I. This thickly armoured infantry tank was used by the BEF at Arras but was available in only small numbers. Model shown is a resin kit from Milicast.

Shown in the unusual Western Desert Caunter scheme, these early war tanks are white metal kits from MMS and Airfix.

This Vickers Mk IV light tank was a kit made by Vulcan Models and in 1/35 scale. Model by Simon Ward.

A9 and A10 Cruiser Tanks of the British Expeditionary Force. White metal 1/76 scale kits from MMS Models. Sadly, this manufacturer has all but disappeared.

Mid-war Armour

By the battle of El Alamein in October 1942 British armoured divisions were composed of not only British-built tanks, like the Crusader, but American tanks supplied under lend-lease, like the Grant and Lee and the Sherman. In the smaller scales these vehicles are available from Airfix, Hasagawa, Mirage and S&S Models. In the larger scales Tamiya, Academy, Meng and Trumpeter (to name but a few) include tanks from this era.

This Crusader Mk I tank is a 1/72 scale metal diecast kit that has been lightly weathered. (Photograph by Alex Cossey)

With a Mirage Models 1/72 scale Grant in the background this diorama shows the crew 'brewing up'. Figures from Dan Taylor Modelworks and Early War Miniatures. (Photograph by Alex Cossey)

American Lee tank from Academy in 1/35 scale. The British used mainly the Grant but did have a few Lee tanks in the 8th Army. Model by Simon Ward.

This Sherman painted in Western Desert camouflage is a resin conversion kit from Matador Models in 1/76 scale. (Photograph by Alex Cossey)

Late War Armour

By the time of the invasion of Italy British armour was mainly the Sherman in the armoured divisions with the infantry supported by the Churchill and Valentine. By the Normandy Invasion in June 1944 a new British medium tank – the Cromwell – made its first appearance. The best armed tank the British had in Normandy was the Firefly armed with a 17 pdr gun. The best British tank of the Second World War was undoubtedly the Comet and, just too late to see active service, the 'Universal Tank' known as the Centurion appeared. This period is well catered for by all kit manufacturers in all scales.

This Churchill Crocodile is a 1/48 scale model built and photographed by Neil McConnachie. Beautifully finished to represent a tank from 79th Armoured Division.

A 1/35 scale Valentine in New Zealand colours built by Mark Gilbert.

Tamiya 1/35 scale Cromwell in a scenic setting with crew from Simon Ward.

A Tamiya 1/48 scale Firefly of 11th Armoured Division built and photographed by Neil McConnachie.

The Centurion Mk I was rushed to Europe in May 1945 but arrived too late to fire a shot in anger. This 1/76 model is by Ben Graves, using a turret from his now sadly discontinued B4 Range. (Photograph by Alex Cossey)

Focus on the Cromwell

The Cromwell tank has often been judged as a poor tank. Pitted against the German Tiger and Panther, it had to close to less than 100 metres to penetrate the armour of the German tanks because of the low velocity 75 mm gun it carried. Whereas the Germans could sit back a kilometre and destroy a Cromwell. Yet once the Allied tanks broke out of the Normandy beaches the Cromwell came into its own. Fast and reliable the Cromwell lead the swift advance to the Falaise pocket and beyond.

The Models

Although an important tank in Britain's armoury, only a few manufacturers have chosen this AFV as their subject. In small scale the first 1/72 scale model was the Revell kit (see Chapter 2). Airfix followed this with a 1/76 version some years later. Arguably one of Airfix's best military vehicle kits, it was their first new AFV in many years and is an excellent model. Wargamers can choose from the Armourfast kit and one from the Plastic Soldier Company. Milicast produce a number of different Cromwells in resin in 1/76 scale. In 1/48 scale Tamiya produce a superb kit. In 1/35 scale Tamiya and Australia-based SKP also produce Cromwells. Finally, the Cromwell kits can be used as the basis for a variety of versions including the ARV or backdated to become a Cavalier. The Cromwell can be adapted, using one of the excellent conversion kits from Dan Taylor Modelworks, into a Centaur, or MMS Models produce a beautifully finished diecast RM Centaur in 1/72 scale. Because small-scale models are relatively cheap, they are a good basis for some AFVs that may or may not have existed. The Comet Crocodile really existed but only as a single prototype.

British armour was not, until recently, well represented in small scale. This 1/76 scale Airfix Cromwell has a crew from AB Figures.

Small-scale models are often associated with wargaming. This Cromwell from Armourfast is in 1/72 scale. (Photograph by Alex Cossey)

The Tamiya 1/48 scale Cromwell goes together well and has a crew from Dartmoor Models. (Photograph by Alex Cossey)

Cromwell ARV, built from Armourfast chassis in 1/72 scale, with conversion parts from Matador Models.

The finished Cromwell armoured recovery vehicle. (Photograph by Alex Cossey)

The Cromwell tank evolved from the Cavalier tank. The Cavalier shown is based on the Airfix Cromwell with a conversion kit from Dan Taylor Modelworks.

This Centaur tank is another diecast model in 1/72 scale from Hobby Master and shows the superb finish including the compass markings around the turret. The model has been weathered to make it look more realistic. (Photograph by Alex Cossey)

After the Second World War a single Comet tank was adapted to carry a flame gun. Unofficially referred to as a Comet Crocodile the tank never went beyond the single prototype. (Photograph by Alex Cossey)

Second World War – German Armoured Vehicles

While the Second World War may be a British obsession, in military modelling circles it is the German AFVs that are the most popular subject, and the shelves of model shops are mainly populated with vehicles from Hitler's Third Reich. The Panther and Tiger series are particularly popular.

Early German Armour

It is a popular myth that the early war success of the Germans was due to superior armour. The truth is that in the Polish campaign most German tanks were lightly armed and armoured Panzer I and Panzer IIs, with some medium Panzer III and even fewer Panzer IV (described at the time as 'heavy' tanks). It was the Blitzkrieg tactics of combining all arms and ground attack aircraft that ensured swift victory.

The Panzer divisions of the Blitzkreig that swept through Poland and then the Low Countries and France mainly consisted of light tanks supported by a few Panzerkampfwage IV. Early Panzer IV Ausf D built by Ben Graves in 1/76 scale.

Mid-war Armour

By 1941, and the war in the Western Desert and the early campaign against the Soviets, the light Panzers were obsolete and versions of the Panzer III and Panzer IV were the main stay of the German armoured divisions. However, early encounters with Soviet T 34, KV 1 and KV 2 showed the Panzers were outclassed. The early Panzers were up gunned and up armoured and supplemented with more heavily armed and armoured tanks in the form of the Tiger, and then the Panther appeared in 1942 and 1943. On all fronts the Panzers were supplemented by assault guns which mounted large guns in the chassis of obsolete tanks. JagdPanzers, and Sturmgeschütz used the chassis of the proven Panzer III and Panzer IV as well as the superb JagdPanther, based on the Panther chassis. An ideal defensive weapon, these AFVs would be used to bolster up Panzer divisions that became depleted as the Second World War progressed.

The Panzer III was the workhorse of the Panzer divisions through the early war period. This Panzer IIIM in 1/72 scale depicts a Panzer II fitted with a low velocity 75 mm gun and used alongside Tiger tanks in Tunisia.

The Panzer IV was up gunned and had increased armour to cope with the evolving threat by Allied tanks on all fronts. Panzer IVF2 from Airfix in 1/76 scale.

One of the final Panzer III was fitted with a high velocity 50 mm gun with armoured skirts (Schürzen). Panzer III L from Revell in 1/72 scale built by Simon Ward.

This 1/76 model is a late version of the venerable Panzer IV series that saw service throughout the Second World War.

The Tiger I made its debut in Tunisia and Leningrad. This early production Tiger is the 1/48 Tamiya kit with some modifications to represent a Tiger used by schwere Panzerabteilung 501. (Photograph by Alex Cossey)

The Jagdpanzer IV, Sd.Kfz. 162, was a German tank destroyer based on the Panzer IV chassis. This later version with the L70 gun was called the Panzer IV/L70. Revell kit in 1/76 scale.

Based on the Panther tank, the JagdPanther was armed with an 88 mm L71 main gun. Revell kit in 1/76 with 'Waffle Plate' zimmerit added.

Late War Armour

By 1944 the German Army had been depleted by five years of warfare. New tanks such as the Tiger II and JagdTiger appeared and, although they were superior to Allied armour on the Western Front and many Soviet tanks on the Eastern Front, they were produced in small numbers that would have little impact. As the war draw to its inevitable conclusion, Hitler claimed that German victory would be assured by 'Wonder weapons'. The Maus and E100 went no further than prototypes but these, along with other 'Paper Panzers', would have been of limited value even if they had been produced in large numbers.

The German Tiger II appeared in Normandy. This atmospheric shot shows a Typhoon overflying the tank. Tiger from Airfix in 1/76 scale by Simon Ward.

The JagdTiger fielded a 128 mm gun in a heavily armoured superstructure. Built in small numbers this model is the Trumpeter 1/72 model built by Simon Ward.

Modelling German AFVs

If you decide to model German Second World War tanks then you will have no problem, regardless of scale or subject, as just about every single version of every German AFV is available in kit form.

Focus on the Tiger

The Tiger Tank is probably the most well-known AFV from the Second World War. When first introduced to the battlefield it weighed in at 56 tons, which was twice the weight of the main tanks of the West (Sherman) and East (T34). It was a formidable opponent with thick armour, a deadly 88 mm gun and a reasonable cross-country performance. Fortunately for the Allies, only 1,347 were built between August 1942 and August 1944 (compard to 49,234 Shermans and 84,070 T34s). So, although it took on average three Shermans to destroy a Tiger, there were thirty-seven Shermans and sixty-two T34s for each Tiger fielded. 'Tiger Terror' was a recognised phenomenon in Normandy among Allied tank crews and in the modern model-making fraternity it is perhaps the most popular subject. At one time Dragon produced sixty-five different kits and diecast models of the Tiger in a variety of scales. It is only natural to research the subject that you are building a model for, either to ensure accuracy or just out of interest in the subject. Stories of desperate actions by Panzer crews against impossible odds can easily seduce the reader into believing that these crews were supreme soldiers nothing short of heroes. Yet it is a dangerous path. Tiger tank crews were among the elite, but they were invariably the most fanatical of Nazis. Dedicated to their Fuhrer and ruthlessly cruel. So, while building your model Tiger it's important to recall that if the men who manned those tanks had been successful, the world would be a very different and certainly much darker place.

The Models

Early Tigers
Although the Tiger changed in the two years of production, with the exception of the suspension the changes were only minor. The Tiger had an inauspicious introduction to combat on the Eastern Front near Leningrad and in Tunisia.

Mid-production Tigers
The main change from the early production tanks included replacing one of turret pistol ports with an escape hatch and removal of the Feifel air cleaning system. Some units removed outer road wheels to stop the suspension units clogging up. There were other changes but very minor and sometimes carried out in the field.

Late Production Tigers
The last production Tiger is easily recognised by the all steel wheels, rather than ones with rubber tyres. The Commanders cupola was also radically changed with a hatch cover that slide rather than open on hinges.

Kits of the Tiger tank appear in great profusion. This is a Tamiya 1/48 scale model.

A mid-production Tiger I in 1/48 scale from Tamiya in winter camouflage. Crew figures from Dartmoor Models. (Photograph by Alex Cossey)

A late production Tiger I. Easily identified by the all-steel road wheels and new cupola. Another 1/48 scale kit from Tamiya. (Photograph by Alex Cossey)

Modern Tanks

The period after 1945 to today has been an era of evolving technology and this is very apparent in armoured warfare. All models in this chapter are by Mark Gilbert unless otherwise indicated.

British Armour in the Post-war World

Europe settled into an uneasy peace with the defeat of Germany and Japan in 1945. Although the Soviets had liberated many countries in what would become the Eastern Block, for many it signaled nothing more than a change from one dictator to another. In the post-war world tanks that had served at the end of the Second World War, like the British Churchill, Sherman Firefly and Super Sherman, would continue to serve with some oddities, like the Tortoise Assault Tank appearing in small numbers. But the mainstay of British armour from 1946 was the Centurion, and the 'Cent' remained in British Army service as a main battle tank until replaced by the Chieftain in the late 1960s. While the Western Allies had a superb tank in the Centurion, rising tension with the Soviets led to the development of an AFV that could take on Soviet and Warsaw Pact tanks, like the late Second World War Josef Stalin IS 3 T54, T55 and T62 tanks at long range. Experimental tank destroyer based on the Centurion were (for good reason) never developed. But the Conqueror Heavy tank was more successful with 185 being produced. Development of a replacement for the Centurion began in the 1950s and resulted in the Chieftain.

In the 1980s there was a revolution in tank design when composite armour (also known as Chobham armour) first appeared with the British Challenger tank, the American M1 Abrams and German Leopard 2 tanks. Changes in modern technology have further influenced tank design and the superiority of the new generation of armour was clearly demonstrated in the Gulf Wars.

Modern Model Tanks

There are vast numbers of kits of modern armour available in all scales. Armour of all nations from the entire era is covered by the main kit manufacturers. There has recently been an upsurge in military modelling from countries in Eastern Europe, including Russia, with the prolific company Zvezda. Where there are gaps these are filled the small producers like Model-Miniature from France.

Post-war Churchill Mk IX tank in Irish service.

Mark Gilbert's model of the Sherman Firefly, as used by the Lebanon Christian Militia.

Although heavily modified, the roots of the Sherman tank are still obvious in this M51 as used by the Israeli Army.

Too late to see service in the Second World War, the appropriately named Tortoise carried a 32 pdr gun but the six vehicles built in 1946 never fired a shot in anger.

Britain rushed the Centurion to the front line in the dying days of the Second World War. This model of a Centurion Mk I depicts the AFV as used by Jordan.

The Centurion Mk III in British Army service was fitted with 20 pdr and had two stowage positions for track links on the glacis plate. Model depicts a vehicle used in the Suez conflict.

Very similar to the Mk III the Centurion Mk V had Browning machine guns fitted coaxial to the main gun and in the commander's cupola.

Soviet IS 3 appeared at the Battle for Berlin in 1945 and the low profile, thick armour, and powerful 122 mm gun made it a significant threat to the western allies.

To counter the threat from the Soviet and Warsaw Pact the British developed tank destroyers based on the Centurion chassis. The Conway shown here was one variant.

The FV4005 was armed with a 183 mm gun in an enormous turret. Fitted with a recoil spade, this AFV never went beyond two prototypes.

The Caenarvon combined the FV 201 chassis with a Centurion turret. The FV 201 was eventually developed into the Conqueror.

The Conqueror was a heavy tank designed to destroy Soviet tanks at long range with its 120 mm gun.

The FV 4202 was used to develop various concepts later used in the Chieftain main battle tank.

The front line of the Cold War included the divided city of Berlin. The Chieftains of the Berlin Infantry Brigade sported an unusual urban camouflage scheme. Airfix 1/76 scale Chieftain with Matador Models detailing kit (KCB 47). (Author's collection)

The Chieftain underwent significant changes during its service life. This Mk XI shows the upgrade to 'Still Brew' armour.

Model of the proposed anti-aircraft variant of the Abrams MBT. Equipped with two 35 mm Bushmaster Mk III cannons and an ADATS missile launcher, it was designated M1Air-Ground Defence System. Model by Alan Brown.

Where Next?

We live in an information world. Almost all model makers have access in some form to the World Wide Web and the amount of information for military model makers there is colossal. The following list of websites that I regularly use was accurate when this was written (July 2019).

Clubs and Associations

Miniature Armoured Fighting Vehicle Association: www.mafva.org
International Plastic Modelling Society: https://ipmsuk.org

Online Forums:

Airfix Tribute Forum: www.tapatalk.com/groups/airfixtributeforum
Missing Lynx Forum: www.tapatalk.com/groups/missinglynx/braille-scale-discussion-group-f47210

Small Scale Sites

Henk of Holland. Great site for reviews: http://henk.fox3000.com/index2.htm
Plastic soldiers: www.plasticsoldierreview.com
Small-scale AFVs: www.smallscaleafv.com

Model Kit Manufacturers

Airfix: www.airfix.com/uk-en
Armourfast: www.armourfast.com
Dan Taylor Modelworks: www.dantaylormodelworks.com
Dragon: www.dragon models.com
Friendship Models: www.ebaystores.co.uk/Friendship-Models/Wee-Friends.html
IBG: www.ibg.com.pl
Italeri: www.italeri.com
Mirage Models: www.mhshop.pl

Matador Models: www.matadormodels.co.uk
Milicast: www.milicast.com
Revell: www.revell.com/index.php
Zvezda catalogue:
www.themodellingnews.com/2017/12/zvezdas-new-items-for-2018-in-their.html

Museums

The Tank Museum – Bovington: www.tankmuseum.org/home
The Muckleburgh Collection: www.muckleburgh.co.uk
North Norfolk Tank Museum: www.norfolktankmuseum.co.uk
Imperial War Museum – Duxford: www.iwm.org.uk/iwm-duxford/about

The Printed Word

New books on military modelling and military vehicles appear on an almost daily basis, so it is impossible to record more than a fraction here, but below is a list of my favourite books that I often refer to:

Clark, Alex, *Small Scale Armour Modelling* (Osprey, 2011)
If, like me, you model in small scale, this is the definitive guide and any book by world class model maker Alex Clark is a useful source of information.

Zaloga, Steven, *Modelling US Armour of World War 2* (Osprey, 2009)
Steven J. Zaloga is a military historian, renowned model maker and author who has produced many books on the subject. All are worth a read.

Taylor, Dick, *Warpaint – Colours and Markings of British Army Vehicles 1903–2003*
   (Mushroom Model Publications, 2003)
This is volume 1 in a series by Dick Taylor that is the definitive guide on the subject.

New Vanguard Series

The Vanguard Series from Osprey Publications first appeared in 1977 and the series was revived with the New Vanguard series recently. A lavishly illustrated text is accompanied by beautifully crafted colour illustrations in most of the books from world authorities like David Fletcher Dick Harley and Steve Zaloga.

Images of War

It is a constant source of wonder that although tanks first appeared on the battlefield 100 years ago, new photographs of vehicles from every era (but particularly the Second World War) appear on a weekly basis. This series of books from Pen & Sword Military contains rare and often unseen photographs that are very useful for military model makers.

World War II AFV Plans by George Bradford

This is a series of books that contain scale drawings of Armoured Fighting Vehicles. Mostly centred on the Second World War the drawings are mainly in 1/35 scale with two volumes in 1/72 scale.

Tankcraft Series

Another good series of books from Pen & Sword Military. Aimed at the military modeller, the books are a comprehensive to a specific vehicle type in a particular campaign. All of the series are useful books but those from the pen of Dennis Oliver are particularly well researched.

Commercial Magazines

The magazine racks in most newsagents will contain at least one magazine devoted to model making. The most popular military model making magazines are:

AFV Modeller: www.afvmodeller.com
Military Modelcraft International: www.militarymodelcraft.co.uk/
Military Modelling International: www.pocketmags.com/military-modelling-magazine
Scale Military Modeller International: www.sampublications.com/webshop/scale-military-modeller-international/

Last Words

I hope you have enjoyed this book. It is a very broad subject and the book evolved as I wrote it. I hope the reader can forgive my self-indulgence in the first chapter but know that for some (of a certain age) the hobby was a big influence on our early lives. Returning to the hobby my life has been enriched in so many ways. My skills have improved with time, but I am the first to admit that compared to the likes of Alex Clark and Steve Zaloga I still have much to learn. It may seem strange but building models is only one facet of the hobby. I have met many like-minded people through the hobby and am privileged to call many of them friends. I have regular contact with many of them and seldom do we miss the opportunity to 'Talk Tank'. Social media is also a great tool and although I resisted the pull of Facebook (other social networking services are available), I am now slightly addicted to some of the specialist military modelling pages.

Whether you are new to the hobby or, like me, returning after a long absence, I hope you enjoy the journey as much as I have to date. I say journey because the hobby is a journey of discovery and as you build more and more kits your skills and techniques will improve with time. Don't get frustrated if your models do not look as good as those on the glossy pages of the latest magazine. Throughout this book I have tried to emphasise that the hobby is about developing your own style. Be proud of what you have achieved but most of all enjoy this fantastic hobby that we share.

It would be wrong not to acknowledge those that have helped with the production of this book, apologies for any that I will inevitably miss. Alex Cossey for his amazing photographs (he will go far), Mark Gilbert for his inspiring modern vehicles and allowing me to photograph them. Simon Ward for sharing his vast knowledge. Steve Parsons for being the most inspirational man on the planet. Social Media star Neil McConnachie for allowing me to print some of his 1/48 scale pictures. Connor Stait for his advice and endless patience. Paul Middleton for being Paul Middleton. My children for their continuing support 'oh dad not another book!', and of course to my dearest Karen who, when the dishes needed washing and the grass needed cutting, allowed me to disappear into the study (man cave) to alternatively shout at the computer because it had spelt something wrong (again), or at the airbrush that was clogged.

For Steve.